With our warmest
greetings
Uppsala Domkyrkokör

Exploring Uppsala

Photo: Hasse Schröder

Text: Tore Frängsmyr and Christer Åsberg

Schröders Ord & Bildbyrå AB

Notes: In many respects, it does a disservice to the reader to translate the names of places and people. While the Swedish names of many geographical destinations are very descriptive, the English-speaking tourist would never find them on maps, by asking directions or puzzling together the elements into the total picture. Other names and places have been titled during the years when Latin was the international language. These names are with us today and offer no signs of being changed. The ending -um for the names of buildings denotes a singular neuter genus in Latin. Lineage in the royal family is shown in the middle of the title, not at the end. Thus, Gustaf Adolf the Second is Gustaf II Adolf. We have chosen to stay true to the spelling the visitor will meet in Sweden ... most of the time. Thus, St. Lars remains Lars, not Lawrence. The saintly Birgitta remains Birgitta, not Brigid in a Celt-Anglo revision.

Now for some exceptions that disprove the rule. It can be helpful to know that Östra Ågatan is East River Road, on the east side of the river and the river runs north to south.

Of course some names will be difficult with å, ä and ö. These vowels were added to Swedish to aid in pronunciation, and offer some wonderful additional tools for creators of tongue-twisters, songs, poetry and limericks.

Some terms which re-occur and are translatable are:
Lund = grove or copse. Odinslund, the grove of Odin.
Torg = square or market place.

Exploring Uppsala
© *Photo*   Hasse Schröder 1998, 2001, 2004
© *Text*   Tore Frängsmyr and Christer Åsberg 1998, 2001, 2004

Translation   Margaret Knipe, ABridge

Design   Hasse Schröder
Pre-press   Text & Bild i Motala AB
Printed by   NRS Tryckeri, Jönköping

Schröders Ord & Bildbyrå AB, Gråbergsvägen 2, 752 40 Uppsala
Tel 018 – 55 55 50, Fax 018 – 55 55 56, e-mail hschrode@algonet.se

Third edition

ISBN 91-973551-6-X

Table of Contents

Christer Åsberg

Along the River

Welcome to Uppsala!

At Flottsund, just about 10 km south of Uppsala, the waterway travelling from Lake Mälar (Mälaren) to the sea meets the old road to Stockholm. Arrivals and departures occur here. It was at this junction that Erik XIV, in pomp and circumstance came to be crowned in June 1561. And it was at Flottsund's inn that Glunten and Magistern took an anguished leave from each other in *"Gluntarne"*, (a famous cycle of student songs).

Traffic on the small bridge is less now due to the E 4 which stretches east of the large forest Lunsen. And the impressive oak, which shaded the place where the road turned towards Flottsund is only a dried-out stump and the replacement is a young 25-year old sapling, which none of us will live to see in its full glory.

The boats, which continue up the Fyris River, are certainly more than one would have thought but there is little passenger traffic. Passenger boat traffic was first the responsibility of Olof Rudbeck during the later half of the 1600s while he also managed everything else in Uppsala, from botanical, medical and linguistic research to waterways, bridge construction and fire protection. Steamboat lines to Stockholm started during the 1830s. A limited cargo trade continues today, but mostly it is leisure sailboats passing by. Steamboats, which glide by, are on their way to Skokloster and invite passengers to shrimp feasts during the pleasant trip to Ekoln.

There are many ways to travel to Uppsala, but the most pleasant is always by water. As Ulf Peder Olrog once sang:

To sail around on river Fyris on board a submarine,
I say, that would be something fine for me.

The peculiar name Fyris came from the name given to the fields along the riverbanks on the way to Uppsala called "fören" in Swedish.

The Fyris River at Flottsund.

Kungsängen (The King's Meadow)

At the end of May, masses of the red, white or violet King's Meadow Lily (kungsängsliljor, *Fritillaria meleagris*) bloom along the marshy meadows south of town and above the widening of the Fyris River into large ponds called the Upper and Lower Föret. The lily is the Uppland Province flower and camps together with heaven's birds: Lapwings, kingfishers, blue heron and many others. An Uppland poet, Olof Thunman, names the King's Meadow in a song:

> *Summer approaches the marsh "fören"*
> *And the slowly receding river.*
> *Larks and plovers join in a choir*
> *And bird cherry and blackthorn are in bloom.*

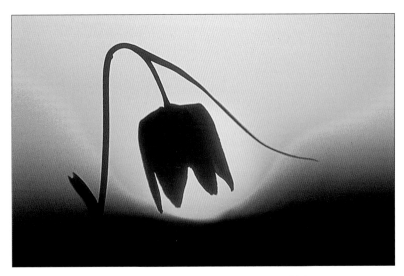

> *Rising out of the clay is an army of lilies*
> *Millions in violet with a dash of white*
> *And the ridge's cuckoos entice and answer*
> *And clouds float far and free.*

It was here that the legendary battle at the Fyris embankment between Erik Segersäll and Styrbjörn Starke took place. For every soldier slain on the battlefield, one lily grew: red for a Dane, white for a Swede. (However, the lily was probably brought here first during the 1800th century). The characteristic silhouettes of the castle and cathedral can be glimpsed through the lilies to the west of the river, completed by a mill along the harbour and other industrial buildings on the east side.

Christer Åsberg

Uppsala Harbour

Steamboats from a bygone era of greatness are still in operation but now as restaurants and tourists boats. Uppsala is a sailor's town, but the marinas are south of town at Ekoln. Freight boats are minimal and the customs house, with functionalist architecture has been made into an elegant office centre.

Iceland's waterfall

Fyris River's last waterfall on the way to the sea is at Island or Iceland. The name comes from the days when flooding would turn the low lying lands around the waterfall into ice in late winter. Now the water flows with a stricter discipline over the damn between the Vershus or Poetry House on the east and the Pump House on the west. About 100 years ago, the Nyblom family lived in the former and a hydroworks was located in the Pump House, now a museum of local technology. Both buildings bear witness in different ways to the importance of the harbour area. Island's waterfall is the destination for the Walpurgis Eve celebrations, shooting the rapids. The concrete bridge spanning over the falls, while not beautiful, is decorated with Olof Hellström's strict, decorative iron railing. Hellström lives in one of the wooden houses near the bridge and has for several decades left his mark on Uppsala with a great number of large and small beautiful and inspiring sculptures, frescoes and mosaics.

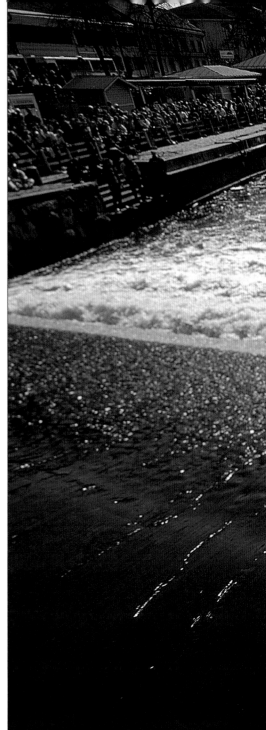

Engineering students arrange shooting the rapids in the morning of April 30 every year. Beauty points are scored for building a float, which makes it to Iceland's waterfall without disintegrating.

Christer Åsberg

At Svandammen (The Swan Pond)

Flustret is the name of an old eatery with accents of ornate decorative carvings for the summer restaurant. Students came here in droves – and thus the name – the gangplank into a beehive is called a "fluster" in Swedish. The restaurant is next to the Stadspark where paths along the Fyris River begin. On the way to the end of the walk at Kap, the walker passes the Students' sport area which has the highest visitors record at the end of March during the Bandy finals.

In front of Flustret is the Swan Pond where well-fed ducks sometimes have the company of students taking a dip. The whole area towards town was formerly a part of the castle's vegetable garden, which was landscaped on top of an area abandoned during the Black Death. Under the castle ridge was a spa with rejuvenating water and some of the pavilions still remain which are used for drinking as companionably but probably less healthy drinks.

Flustret.

The castle crowns the ridge above Svandammen (Swan Pond).

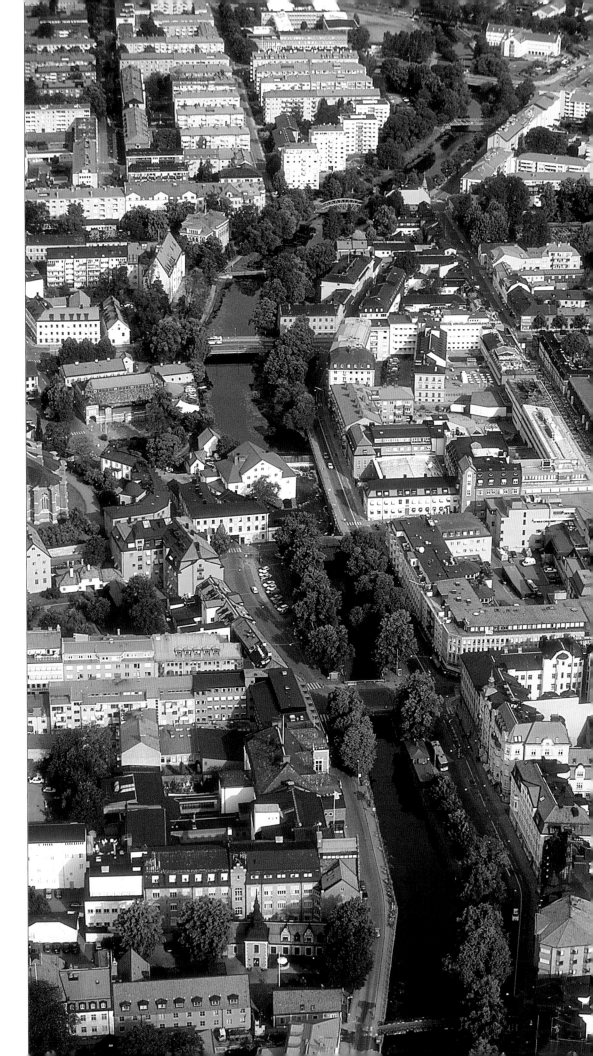

Before Olof Rudbeck's era, the Fyris river was known as Sala river. It has been a line of demarcation between the academic (west side) and the middle-class (east side) Uppsala. But it is also the unifying bond. Uppsala residents have been joined by their sewers, their bathhouse, and their ice-skating course. And the newly renovated "Å-rummet," the name given immediate areas along the river, now features tempting and varied paths for promenades on both sides of the river.

Next pages: *To the west of the Fyris River is the Castle, the University Library, the Cathedral and most of the University institutions.*

At the southern tip of Västra Ågatan (West River Road) is Anatomicum (Asgård). Medicine was taught in the two buildings from 1850 and 1881 for 100 years. Today, lectures are still heard, mainly in psychology. Classes are also held in the attached building from the 1930s.

Laboratorium Chemicum, built in 1753, was crowned with its mansard roof in the style of an estate. During the 1800s, a book printer was situated here and inbetween the World Wars, the Race Biology Institute. The psycology researchers who now populate the area are of a more enlightened school.

"... an old building, 15 windows from left to right and 4 vertically is Olympen. During the many generations of students, much drinking went on, intensive studies, a bit of scientific work and dreams of the future. But, the building was mostly a home for families with doorbells, nameplates and iceboxes." Ture Nerman in the novel Olympen*, 1913. At that point, the building had been there for 60 years.*

Saint Lars Catholic Church from 1985. The Community's head office facing the river reminds one of the architecture of the previous student quarter. The parish has about 2 400 members from 70 countries.

Östra & Västra Ågatan (East and West River Streets)

Östra Ågatan (East River Street)

In Uppsala's youth, the Fyris River was a washing tub and a watering place for livestock. Borgarhusen (middle-class housing) was one block away on Kungsängsgatan and the properties stretched their way to the river with huts, sheds and gardens.

A noteworthy change took place around the mid-1800s. Östra Ågatan became the most coveted address, filled with patrician homes, a street to be seen adorned with stone docks with cast iron fences and luscious

Västgöta nation *was adorned with its castle-like façade in 1901. The building was erected in 1666 and still today, one of the cellar vaults built during the middle ages is being used. The house in the yard is called Ambrosia (food of the gods) after a mess hall that was there during the early part of the 20th century.*

Kaniken, *a commercial office palace was built in a national romantic style in 1913. Up until the 1970s, it housed Almqvist & Wiksell Printers; now Upplands Radio, several other radio stations and, Filmstaden with over a dozen cinemas.*

Norrlands nation *was built in 1889 and reminds one of a Roman villa along the Tiber. Counted in number of members, Norrlands nation is the largest of the 13 nations. Behind the façade are the extensive additions made during the 1970s.*

horse chestnut trees. Several wooden buildings from that time still decorate the area, the most notable being the house of the goldsmith Hellman, with three floors and a front gable.

Next to these wooden houses, one can glimpse the functionalist building which replaced the notorious students' inn. The better known buildings are the Hotel Hörnan and the block named Nightingale where a local morning newspaper was printed between 1907-58. Uppsala's oldest coffee house, Güntherska, is still going strong. The Lundequistska bookstore has moved to make room for the new Upplands Bank.

Fyristorg (Fyris Square)

The site of Uppsala's first hospital erected by Dean Andreas
And in 1302 is now Fyris Square. Exactly 400 years later,
Uppsala burned to the ground and the new square was
made. With the advent of the car, the square became a
source of traffic problems. In the 1930s, a passageway
was cut through the Gillberg building on the north side.
During Glunten's and Magistern's time (two literary
students famous for carousing), there were many pubs
along Fyris Square. Perhaps both were on their way to the
pubs when their walk ended hastily by the night-watch-
man at Dombron
(Cathedral Bridge)
during the famous
Night March in
Saint Erik's alley.

The Gillet Hotel
with the town's most
famous restaurant
was located in the
Square's largest build-
ing until 1972. In
the southern corner,
there used to be a
bulletin board for
general notices and

16

Östra Ågatan (East River Street) following the Fyris River.

posters. People would loiter and discuss giving the place the name Politiska knuten (Political corner), which has survived the bulletin board.

On Friday nights, the square is invaded by teenagers in hot-rods till the vendors arrive in the morning.

Dombron (Cathedral Bridge) and book sellers

Next pages:
Dombron (Cathedral Bridge) on a very cold winter morning.

Saturday along the Fyris River.

Of the dozen bridges connecting the east and west sides of the Fyris River, Dombron (Cathedral Bridge) is the oldest starting at the Old Square. A bridge has been here since the 1200s but the stone bridge now is from 1760. The graceful arch is best seen from Fyris Square's other bridge, which is almost as old but has the name of New Bridge (Nybron) from an extensive renovation at the end of the last century. Between the bridges on Östra Ågatan, Uppsala's second-hand bookstores have taken after their Parisian colleagues and have their stalls underneath the chestnut trees when weather, wind and police allow.

Akademikvarnen (The Academy Mill)

A key point in Uppsala is the area around the Mill water-fall. One could wade across the Fyris River here and the fall loaned its power to the mill, to hammers and saws. According to legend, Saint Erik was murdered here in 1160, and "where his blood ran out a spring did cometh". Saint Erik's spring it is called still and is commemorated by an impressive bronze tower from the 1850s.

On the Mill islet, the oldest mill was built during the 1280s. The benefactor, Andreas And, bequeathed his house to Uppsala to be used for theology students several decades later. Thus the islet also has the name Student islet.

As late as the 1800s a ferry boat navigated above the Mill Falls. Several other stretches along the river had ferry traffic as a complement to the few bridges.

The mill changed hands in the 1600s when the church transferred it to the university as a part of Gustaf II Adolf's attempt to strengthen the university's finances. The mill was active until 1946. In the old mill house with

The cathedral was built at the centre of the market place, on the heights above the Mill Falls. The cathedral was ringed in by various buildings. The original pattern can be seen today, though the buildings are

Green lawns, privacy, room to stretch and a cup of coffee. Right in the middle of town!

later. The tower with its dome houses Nathan Söderblom's library.

The dean's residence is in one of the surrounding buildings. Church offices, the university and artisans occupy the others.

traditions dating from the 1700s, a new Uppland Museum was created in 1959. While the building has been used for peaceful ends, flour milling and culture, its impressive, strict architecture created the perfect environment for the despotic bishop in Ingmar Bergman's film, *Fanny and Alexander*.

On Walpurgis Eve, students shooting the rapids in their fragile, decorated vessels can be seen on the river near Fjellstedt's school, before these are destroyed by the white water. At the beginning of the century, other battles were fought here. The section of river between Fjellstedt's and YMCA (KFUM) was the home arena for the team IFK Uppsala, which has been Swedish master in bandy 12 times.

The Iron Bridge and Alfvén Hall

The Iron Bridge contributes to the city's beauty. Since 1987 it has been for pedestrian and bicycle traffic between St. Johannesgatan and Linnégatan. Prior to 1964, it was located one block to the south where Saint Olof's Bridge now spans the river. It was removed but after 23 years it was raised again, much to the delight of city residents. The bridge was first called Prince Carl's bridge, after the future Carl XV. Construction began in 1846 as a work project for unemployed, with the intention of "creating a contribution to the area's suffering inhabitants".

The magnificent building, which was built in 1911 by the YMCA, is still called the YMCA stronghold. In addition to flats, the building houses the choir Orphei Drängar (OD). The old gym hall is restored to its original Art Nouveau style and renovated for concerts, choirs and smaller ensembles. It has been named the Alfvén Hall after Hugo Alfvén, OD's conductor for many years.

Fjellstedt's Boardwalk

Between the Iron Bridge and Saint Olof's Bridge is the
building which housed Fjellstedt's School between
1880–1982. It was a school for the Swedish Church giving
indigent boys from the whole country the possibility to
study for the priesthood.

   It is possible to walk along the length of the river in the
city. A newly built boardwalk outside of the old school
has quickly become a popular meeting place for the city's
youth.

There are no traces of Valsgärde's belligerent past. Uppsala's airfield lies between the city and Valsgärde. The Air Force base F 16 came into being during the war years and was closed down at the end of 2003. The Air Force Military Academy has survived as F 20 and, in the future, a number of upper management will be placed here. Nearby is also a little civilian flying field for gliders and small airplanes.

Valsgärde

There was history before Uppsala. In Gamla Uppsala, one experiences a strong tie to the pagan past. The three royal mounds create the impression that the old church is a bit modern. A few kilometres north of Gamla Uppsala is Valsgärde (gärde = field). Here is a timeless idyll. On the slopes approaching the river can be seen here and there about 10 metre long depressions. The local chieftains, farmer leaders, and soldiers were placed in boats which were pulled up on land and then buried with a protective building above them. When this collapsed, the resulting form was of a boat. This type of burial differs from that of Old Uppsala where the gravesites were burned. Diggings have thus yielded rich artefacts, above all weapons, helmets and shields, but also kitchen utensils and other necessary tools for the last voyage. Most of the graves are from the Viking era, but some are from the Vendel era (550–800). This was named after the parish Vendel, farther up the

Fyris River. The fascinating aspect is that the burial mounds were used for perhaps 15 generations, which gives evidence to an unusually stable chieftainship on the outpost of the Svea kingdom.

We have followed the winding Fyris River through Uppsala. To make the same trip by car or bike means a 30 kilometre long perfectly straight road from Flottsund to Ärna and farther up to Björklinge. This road was laid when Uppsala had a new town plan in 1643. Uppsala should be a modern and stately European city.

Next pages:
The mounds in Gamla Uppsala have been here for 15 centuries.

Christer Åsberg

How did Uppsala come to be?

The royal mounds in Gamla Uppsala.

A river estuary, called aros in Old Swedish, was always a very important meeting place for travel and commerce, and thereby a natural place for religious cults, political power centres and military manoeuvres.

During the Viking era, people came to Uppsala via the Långhundra channel from the Baltic Sea or by the Mälar channel from Birka. Both of the waterways came together at "Aros", the river estuary that is now the centre of Uppsala. The Fyris River was called Sala Å then, and could be navigated a bit farther than possible today. About 5 km up-river, the town of Uppsala was located and means "up above Sala." During the 500s, the era of the Great Migration, people buried their rulers in mounded graves: Ane the elder, his son Egil and grandson Adils. Sala was a village east of Aros, or, according to other opinions, the king's lands, barns, or "halls", near the seat of the cult in Uppsala.

The rising of the land created a new shelf in the Fyris River at the mill waterfall at Dombron. There the roads from Dalarna and Norrland, from Västerås (Västra Aros) and Roslagen met. During the 1100s, this meeting place had increased its economic importance. In the 1160s, coins were minted in the new Uppsala. At the same time, an archbishop was named to a seat in Gamla Uppsala. But, in the 1200s, even the church moved to the new Uppsala.

Soon, Aros became Uppsala while the former Uppsala became Gamla or Old Uppsala. In an agreement with the church in 1286, King Magnus Ladulås allowed "fishing under the bridge in Aros, now called Uppsala, and half of the river from the named fishing site up unto the end of the mill". Uppsala's history begins from that year.

Gamla Uppsala late in winter in the middle of the 1000s:

"Of all men and beasts of male sex, 9 are offered, and the blood from the sacrificed is used to appease the gods. The bodies are hung upside down in a grove near the temple. This grove is regarded by the pagans to be so holy that every tree is thought to have godly attributes as a result of the dead and rotting bodies of the sacrificed. Horses, dogs and humans hang there, and one of the

Christians has told me that he has seen 72 bodies hanging there one after another. They sing songs over and over, which is common with these holy sacrificial ceremonies, but these are obscene and are best kept secret."

The above is from *History of the Hamburg Diocese and its Bishops* (1070s) by Adam of Bremen. Experts are still arguing about the reporting and if the scenes described really occurred as Adam states.

Christer Åsberg

Rune Stones

The area around Uppsala has more rune stones than any other region in Sweden. Most of the stones were raised and inscribed during the 1000s. These were historical markers indicating road-building or bridge construction or for someone who died in bed, or on a raid overseas. Many rune stones have been removed from their place of origin and used as fill in new buildings in town before being re-discovered in our own time. One stone from Rasbo was used to decorate an archaeologist's garden during the 1700s and lay at the bottom of Le Havre's harbour after being viewed at the World's Exhibition in Paris. Now it parades together with other stones in the University Park. Others can be seen in the walls or floors of the Cathedral, and others are found along country roads and fields.

The most beautiful rune stones were engraved by Öpir. The rune stones reflect the beginning of Christendom in Sweden. Tor's Hammer was eventually exchanged for the Christian cross. That so many of the areas´ powerful leaders during the 1000s converted to Christianity has led researchers to question whether Old Uppsala was, in fact, a heathen cultural centre.

Next pages:
The church and the royal burial mounds in Gamla Uppsala.

Rune stones found in the University park and around Uppsala.

Torgisl and Gisl raised this stone for Sven, their father.

Holmfast raised this stone in memory of Igulger, the father and Torbjörn.

Tjägn and Gunnar raised this stone in memory of Väder, their brother.

… raised this stone in memory of Kettilbjörn, the father, and Runfrid for her husband and Igulfast made possible but Öpir engraved.

The church in Gamla Uppsala

This church was the cathedral until 1273 when the archbishop moved to Uppsala. The central tower and the choir from the original structure still stand, but many restorations have been carried out during its 800-year history. Earlier there was a wooden church. Whether the church was built on the site of a pagan temple is uncertain.

Historical centre

The kings' burial mounds from the 500s have stimulated both serious research and fantasy through the centuries. Sometimes the two tangents have married such as in Olof Rudbeck's work during the 1600s. He proved that the sunken continent Atlantis had its centre just here. An exhibition hall designed by Carl Nyrén was opened in 2000. In this building, designed to resemble an eye, one meets the rich culture heritage from the Vendel period, the helmets of the kings and the clothing worn by priestesses.

Christer Åsberg

The Church in the middle of town

The trading area of Östra Aros developed during the 1100s into a town. Gamla or Old Uppsala was the seat for the archbishop in 1164, but only 100 years later in 1258, the Pope decided to move the residence. It was said that the site of Gamla Uppsala was founded on a "desecrated and wretched site" and that "there was no one to preach the word of God to." So, they moved 5 km south. From Slottsbacken, the royal mounds can be seen and from them, you can discern the new town's characteristic contours.

There are many speculations as to the appearance of the area when the construction began. It now appears that neither a church, fortification nor a surrounding wall were present when the cathedral was built as was the general opinion earlier. There were only simple structures that were ploughed under to make room for the landfill creating the cathedral's plateau. Archeological diggings constantly uncover new information on Uppsala's earlier history and there are great uncertainties.

Next pages:
At Saint Erik's Square.

In the Cathedral's shadow

It is easy to imagine the enormous impression the cathedral
must have made on the little town. Today the eye picks
out the cathedral when nearing town from a distance of
about 10 km. A Cathedral 118,7 meters high and 118,7
metres long cannot disappear easily. Still, from a distance
it is both graceful and slender. Paradoxically, the impression

will be different when moving around in town. From a short distance, the church cannot be viewed in its full glory. One can see bits and pieces of changing, pleasing geometric forms in combination with walls and roofs jutting out from the surrounding buildings which crowd around, but the end result is a moving and lively lasting impression.

The surrounding environment

In January 1273, the archbishop moved his residence from Gamla Uppsala to Östra Aros. The Distings market was approaching so there were many people in town. In a procession filled with pomp and circumstance, Saint Erik's relics were carried to the new resting-place. Construction on the cathedral had already begun. In 1287, a French sculptor arrived. He may have designed the three porches. The Gothic style is somewhat modified after the Dominicans' less showy style and adapted to the Northern climatic condition. Building materials are primarily brick; there are traces of the ovens used for the bricks. This started an industry that has been present until our own time.

Work continued for more than five generations. Uppsala has a tradition of long-drawn out public building projects. The dedication was in 1435, which was the same year as Sweden's first parliament. Among those attending were the author of Song of Freedom, Bishop Tomas and the newly elected national captain, Engelbrekt.

No towers were planned for the cathedral, but soon the two western towers were built and spires added on. The first spires were drawn as early as the 1600s and were much lower than those now. In 1702, fire raged through Uppsala and burned down the cathedral in spite of Olof Rudbeck's heroic attempts to lead fire-fighting.

The Cathedral seems to rise out of the older buildings.

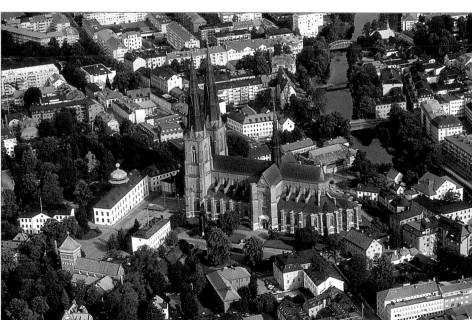

Around the middle of the 1700s, the town was to some extent rebuilt. The towers, which much later Bellman, Geijer and Wennerberg would see as the towers on "their cathedral" were called Hårleman's towers after the architect. These were low and gave the church a hint of the baroque style instead of the original gothic. The church appeared to have shrunk, and the flying buttresses were gone. However, the lower profile melted in well with a town of one- and two story houses.

Saint Erik's Square and Odinslund

Carl Hårleman created the monumental environment from the 1700s on the north side of cathedral hill. Saint Erik's Square became a representative square for trade even though it had the mundane name Oxen Square until 1822. The square's marketing tradition made this the natural site for the first covered market.

Hårleman fixed up Gustavianum and built the university council house. Both of these giants frame the church when one walks out to the square from Saint Lars Street. The Royal Society of Sciences building is on the left and Ekerman's house on the right. The university council house was used for the university's entrance exams during the 1800s.

Trinity Church has been recorded as a parish church for the Bondkyrko, parishioners from the countryside, from 1302 up until 1947, when a reform incorporated the church into the Uppsala diocese. During the 1800s, the parish was a prebend with a theology professor as pastor. Trinity Church is a more comfortable size than the Cathedral for weddings and burials.

The Archbishop's residence sits on a hill between the University and Cathedral.

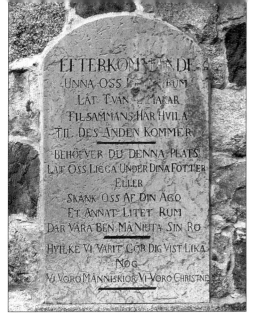

to 1832, the church had its own graveyard.
he rumours that the graveyard would be
oved caused the moving message on the gra-
stone, which is inserted into the church
all:

Generations After Us, Give Us This Place,
et Spouses Together Rest Here Until the
pirit Comes

If You Need This Place Let Us Lie Under-
ath Your Feet Or Share With Us From Your
operty Another Little Place Where Our
nes Can Enjoy Peace.

Who We Were Makes No Difference. We
ere Human Beings. We Were Christians.

ekan House across from the Archbishop's resi-
nce was built on foundations from the middle
es as the Julinsköld palace in 1741. Petter
linsköld was responsible for the university's
ances but privatised without prejudice parts
it to build this magnificent house with 45
oms, all of which could be heated. During
e 1800s, the first Cathedral School was here
d later a seminary, until they were given
eir own buildings in Luthagen.

August Strindberg describes a Latin exam in *Från Fjärd-ingen till Svartbäcken*, 1877. If Petrus Ekerman hadn't been a Latin professor during the 1700s, he could have been taken right out of Strindberg's satire. He took bribes and payments for writing his students' theses. In the grand house his activities financed is now the Department of History.

If we continue around the cathedral going by Gustavianum we come to Odinslund. The name was invented during the 1900s, but a pagan-offering place may have been at Riddartorget (Knight's Square) on the other side of the Dekan House. A tall obelisk was raised here in memory of Gustaf II Adolf in 1832. At the same time, Odinslund received the profile we see today and the graveyard at Trinity Church was moved.

Of the many monuments built by Hårleman from the middle of the 1700s, is the Archbishop's residence. The present resident is KG Hammar. Among his predecessors are Gunnar Hultgren, Yngve Brilioth, Nathan Söderblom and the colourful Anton Niklas Sundberg. In 1837, when Johan Olof Wallin was archbishop for a short time, he discovered his bankrupt predecessor had rented out the residence to the town's salon hostess and gossip, Malla Silferstolpe who generously allowed the archbishop a few rooms.

Below the Dekan House is Riddartorget with Värmlands nation, built in 1930 by Ragnar Östberg. The Oxenstierna House is also here, housing the Law school but from the beginning in 1708, a hospital. Along the southern wall of the church was the first university buil-ding, Academia Carolina, torn down in 1778.

Skytteanum can be seen farther down, donated by Gustaf II Adolf's teacher, John Skytte, dedicated to political

The Archangel Michael on the eastern roof is waiting for a sign that the Day of Resurrection is breaking.

The cathedral is built on land granted by the king. The relationship between state and church has generally been good.

During the late Middle Ages and the Reformation, there were both religious and economic conflicts. The bastion Styrbiskop is a reminder with its row of canons trained on the cathedral and archbishop's residence.

science studies and debate which was the great power's top notch research and best management training centre.

The cathedral's south porch facing Riddartorget is the most detailed. It is dedicated to the priestly saint Saint Lars, the cathedral's patron saint. That the main entrance was in the south was typical for Swedish churches from the Middle Ages: the purpose was for parishioners to gather in a warm, protected place after Mass. The north porch is dedicated to Saint Olof, the Nordic patron saint. In the present day main entrance to the west is Uppsala's own patron saint, Saint Erik who welcomes visitors.

The cathedral was extensively renovated about 100 years ago between 1885–93. The roof leaked causing rot to set in, one of the towers settled, other flaws were obvious. An additional motivation was one of taste. The experts wanted to restore the church to its original Gothic style. Public opinion approved the idea of towers rising high in the sky.

Work began under Helgo Zetterwall and the results were debated. The many small towers, flying buttresses, sculptures, gutters, drains etc with which Zetterwall decorated the church gave it more a cluttered façade than the Gothic style. It was an ill-fated decision to use cement for sealing joints and decorations. The cement cracked, bricks disintegrated, and the roof decorations toppled down. The west porch needed to be protected by a wooden roof.

A new restoration conducted by Åke Porne was finished in 1976. The original Gothic style was once again in place but the exaggerations of the 1890s were erased.

In 2000, the legal bonds between state and church were dissolved. In Uppsala, the traditional free churches are represented. The Mission Church on Saint Olof Street, with its graceful form, is open for all sorts of cultural events. Newer charismatic success theology exported from the US is represented in the Word of Life group, which has its church in Årsta.

The interior of the Cathedral

Before the Assembly of the World
Council of Churches in Uppsala in
1968, Olof Hellström designed a sculpture in iron to hold candles, the Tree of
the Reconciled Peoples. The continents
grow into a tree with candleholders.
The sculpture soon became an area for
meditation for frequent communicants
and also for temporary visitors hesitating
in the doorways, seeking peace and
spiritual experience. To buy a candle,
light it and place it in a candleholder
soon became a churchly tradition, which
quickly spread throughout the country.

East, west, north and south
The arms of the cross cover all

Next pages:
The Cathedral's interior length is 107 metres, 45 metres wide and at the highest point is 27 metres.

Anders Frostenson's psalm gave inspiration to the candle-holder sculpture but also to a large tapestry in one of the side choirs, the Peace chapel, designed by Anna-Lisa Odelqvist-Kruse. Other textile treasures can be seen in the church's museum in the north tower.

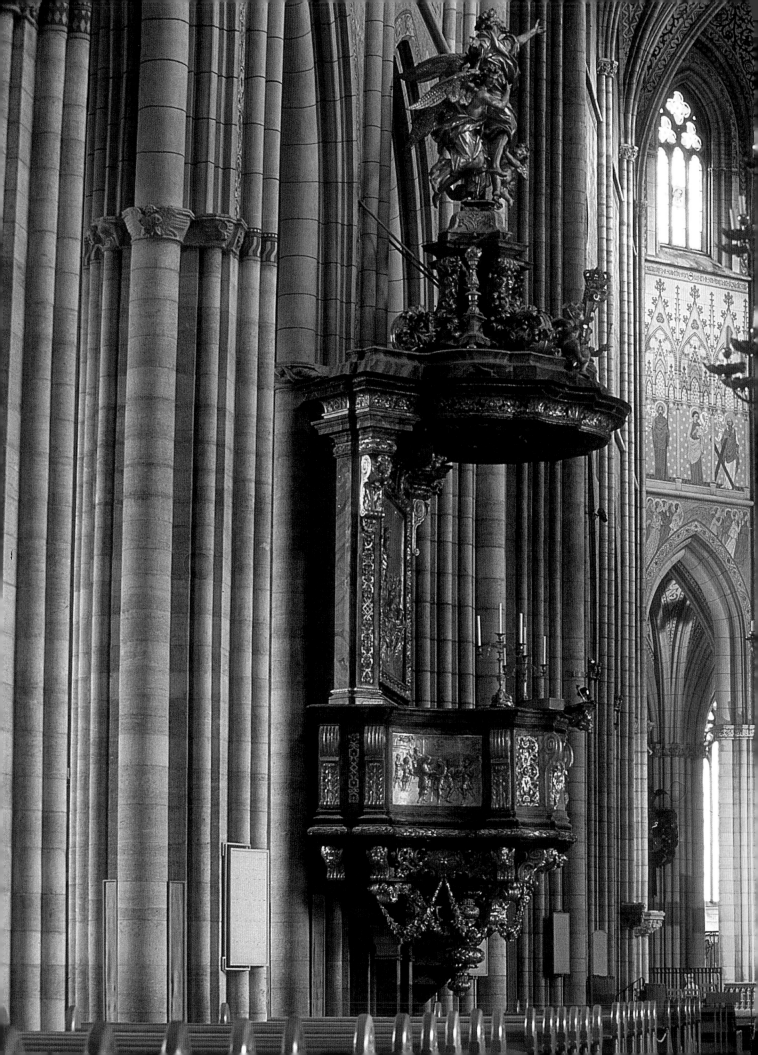

The cathedral has a typically Gothic church style but is unique with its mild and soft light. The windows are placed in such a way so that daylight gives direct light but is also reflected from the arches. The lighting creates an ambience of peace and solemnity and is also advantageous for the 13 000 m² of roof and wall murals.

The façade is mostly brick, but the inside is dominated by limestone from Gotland. The stone masons from Gotland have created sculptures, which illustrate the view from the Middle Age of the virtues and vices. Originally these were colourful. The series includes the much discussed "Jewish sow", which portrays arrogance and is one of the few examples in Sweden of the anti-Semitism from the Middle Ages. The magnificent pulpit was given to the church by the widow Queen Hedvig Eleonora after the fire in 1702. The cross above the high altar was made of silver and glass by Bertil Berggren-Askenström for the re-dedication in 1976.

The cathedral's transept was built first and then the choir. It took 60 years. The remainder of the construction time was spent completing the body of the church. At the point of the cross in middle of the transept, 27 metres up, the final stone was placed, marked with the hand of God in a blessing. Just underneath this is the spot where coronations took place until 1719.

Nathan Söderblom (1866–1933) was a religion historian, church leader, archbishop, psalm composer, member of the esteemed Swedish Academy and much more. He strove to bring about ecumenical co-operation among the Christian churches, understanding and respect between the Church and the new popular movements, and a fruitful dialogue between Christianity and Humanism. His open and enlightened character made a great impression and is still experienced today in the tones he wrote for a well-loved psalm:

> *In the wonderful summer,*
> *Go out, my soul, and be happy for*
> *The gifts of our great God.*
> *See how lovely the world looks*
> *See how for you and me the earth bears wonderful gifts*

Söderblom's statue was raised on the edge of the Archbishop's garden and faces the Decan House, where the Department of Theology was lodged and where he was professor, and also Trinity church, where he was pastor. The little bronze statue was made by Bror Hjorth, who admired Söderblom's work for peace: he was awarded the Nobel Peace Prize in 1930.

Closer to the church and outside of the southern porch is another statue with Söderblom's features. The sculptor Christian Eriksson loaned these in memory of Jacob Ulfsson, archbishop when the university was founded in 1477.

The Finsta Chapel belongs to Birger Persson, St. Birgitta's father. The young Birgitta is portrayed in stone. The Chapel also contains the chest with St. Erik's relics and Sweden's first royal crown. The large, decorated chest is not the same one brought to Uppsala in 1273, but the third one in succession. Johan III ordered a new chest during the 1570s. A memorial plaque on the floor in front of the chest commemorates Pope John Paul's and Archbishop Bertil Werkström's joint prayer for church unity when the Pope visited Uppsala in 1989.

The Lady Chapel behind the high altar was dedicated to the Virgin Mary. But Gustaf Vasa wanted the chapel for his burial vault. He lies here with his first two wives. The sarcophagi portrays the two wives and the king in life-size. The bodies face the east, waiting for the resurrection. The chapel was meant to symbolise Gustaf Vasa's unique role as the unifier of the country and the founder of the dynasty. At his funeral in 1560, his work was compared to the work performed by Jesus and he was granted a place in the illustrious Geatish past. The walls portray events in Gustaf Vasa's history including his entrance into Stockholm in 1523. J.G. Sandberg painted these in 1838.

Katarina Jagellonica was Johan III's Polish-born spouse. She died in 1583, nine years before her husband. Willem Boy, who also made Gustaf Vasa's, formed the

sarcophagus.

Johan III rests on the other side of the chapel. His relaxed posture with one leg crossing the other shows that the monument was to be placed in a nisch with a slight angle. It was properly placed first in 1818 during a renovation. Later, murals portraying scenes from Cracow and Stockholm were painted.

The chapel where both are

buried belongs to the oldest part of the church, the north transept, which was used in the 1200s.

In a side chapel are the remains of Emanuel Swedenborg (1688–1772). He left Uppsala as a famous scientist. By the time his body was returned in 1908 and buried in the cathedral, he was world famous for research in spiritual secrets. The skull uncovered from the coffin was not Swedenborg's. It was first in 1978 the skull was returned and buried with the rest of the remains.

Under a slab of stone to the left of the main entrance is Carl von Linne's (1707–78) final resting place together with his wife and son, the latter who followed in his father's footsteps as a botanist.

Christer Åsberg

More than 200 choirs!

Churches are an important foundation for Uppsala's uniquely rich choir life. The Cathedral Choir was founded as early as 1867. In the cathedral there is a number of smaller vocal ensemble and chorale groups. The Gosskören (Boys Choir) has a special place in the hearts of Uppsala residents, whose concerts on the feast of St. Lucia have long been a great event. Other choirs can be found in the Trinity Church, Vindhems Church, Mission Church and the Catholic church.

A great leap in the quality of the choirs can be attributed to the provincial music schools. The students interested in song now coming to Uppsala have several years of training and education behind them. They can join their talents and abilities with the long-standing choir tradition based

Next page:
Cathedral Choir.

The cathedral's Boys Choir celebrates the feast of St. Lucia in the University Aula.

Photo: Martin Schröder

in a historical perspective, transfer of knowledge and a wonderful way of working together. The most outstanding choirs, such as Allmänna sången and Akademiska kammarkören, have high entrance standards. But, Uppsala has more than 200 choirs; whoever wants to sing in a choir can do it. Choirs appear in churches, in companies, public agencies, in schools, in student nations and in organisations.

But there is other music. The Akademiska Kapellet and Uppsala Kammarorkester offer symphony music. Jazz musicians such as Lars Erstrand and Ulf Johansson-Werre are Uppsala residents and jazz has lately re-established itself. Claes Janson and Viktoria Tolstoy are two singers who have made names for themselves. A number of rock and pop bands from Uppsala have been noticed both nationally and internationally. Every other year, Uppsala hosts the student orchestra festival, STORK.

Orphei Drängar split off from Allmänna sången in 1853 with the purpose of being an elite choir. Eric Ericson, leader since 1951, gave the choir its characteristic to sing the most modern male choir repertoire in all languages — with a great amount of ease. Robert Sund has continued the

Every nation with self-respect has its own orchestra. Wermeslaget belongs to Värmlands nation.

tradition. The elite profile doesn't exclude OD from celebrating triumphs with its soft, tight sound and exact diction in traditional serenades or in the mixed form of serious and jolly performance called Caprice.

Uppsala has much music. What it since long wanted to have is a concert hall, with rooms for ensembles, concerts, rehearsals, library, etc. For many years, groundbreaking has almost been a reality. In April 2004 the City Council eventually decided that a magnificent concert hall shall be built at Vaksala torg.

Next pages:
In the Linné garden.

Tore Frängsmyr

The King's Uppsala

Construction on Uppsala Castle began during the 1540s but strictly speaking was never completed. Gustaf Vasa had several intentions with his castle project. At that time it was common for a king to have castles at different locations in the country. He would live there during visits, his representatives would live there, and the castle would be the judicial, administrative and economic centre for royal power. Castles were often placed at strategic locations so they could also serve as a fortification.

This was also true of Uppsala Castle, Vasaborgen (Vasa stronghold). However, there was an additional factor in Gustaf's planning. Uppsala was the centre of religion by virtue of the cathedral and the Archbishop's residence ever since the 1200s. Here kings were crowned and buried, here the national conclaves took place, ceremonies and celebrations. The king intended to enforce his own power in relation to the Church. This is why he built his castle at a high point on the Uppsala ridge where he also built a castle church.

Both Gustaf Vasa and his sons used the castle, living there while holding meetings, and building additions; a castle is not built in one day.

It was for example here that Erik XIV knifed Nils Sture in May, 1567, and passed the death sentence on five more people. He had begun to suspect his noblemen and resorted to these drastic measures during a fit of mental aberration. After a fire in 1572, Johan III could restore the castle to a more proportional structure. The royal coronation celebrations were held in the large national hall while the common people were treated to a banquet outside in the courtyard.

Next pages:
The western façade of Uppsala Castle. The Gunilla belltower stands on the north bastion, Styrbiskop.

During Gustaf II Adolf's time, the restoration and building of the castle stopped. At that point there was one long and narrow building with a wider wing on the south which ended in a bastion. The north wing was never built, but a low, simple structure was there during a number of years. Even in this direction there was a bastion. There were three towers. In addition to the north and south tower, which still stand today, there was a tower on the southern wing's bastion.

Queen Christina lived for a long time in Uppsala, though she was the first regent to be crowned in Stockholm instead of Uppsala in 1650. Four years later however, she abdicated her throne in Uppsala. After Christina's time, there were restorations and additions. Olof Rudbeck was given the mission to create a castle garden at the front of the castle by Carl XI. In the late 1700s Gustaf III donated the garden to the University and it is now the Botanical Garden.

In 1702, the Castle fell victim to the fire which left much of Uppsala in ashes. The Castle was uninhabitable but some parts could be used including the jail. The architect Carl Hårleman was commissioned to restore the Castle in 1744. He shortened the south wing giving it the form we see today, and planned to do the same for the north wing. This was never realised. Rooms with high ceilings were divided into several rooms with a lower

A garden in the Baroque style was planned to the west of the castle. It is now the Botanical Garden.

ceiling; in this way, the old castle church disappeared. Much of the tiles and other building materials were transported to Stockholm to aid in Hårleman's restoration of Stockholm's Castle.

Terraces were etched into the side of the ridge from the garden up to the castle. The lower parts of the terraces were used as a transport road for masonry and other building materials when the University Library, Carolina Rediviva, was to be built during the 1840s. Thus a road came into existence which still separates the castle from the garden. Earlier it was called the Stockholm Road but was renamed Dag Hammarskjöld's Road after the United Nations General Secretary who grew up in the castle where his father was the county governor.

Today the castle is used as the residence for the county governor. The national hall, restored in 1932, is used for banquets for conferment of doctoral degrees and other solemn occasions. Extensive restorations have been carried out in later years including the remaining south wing now open for tourists.

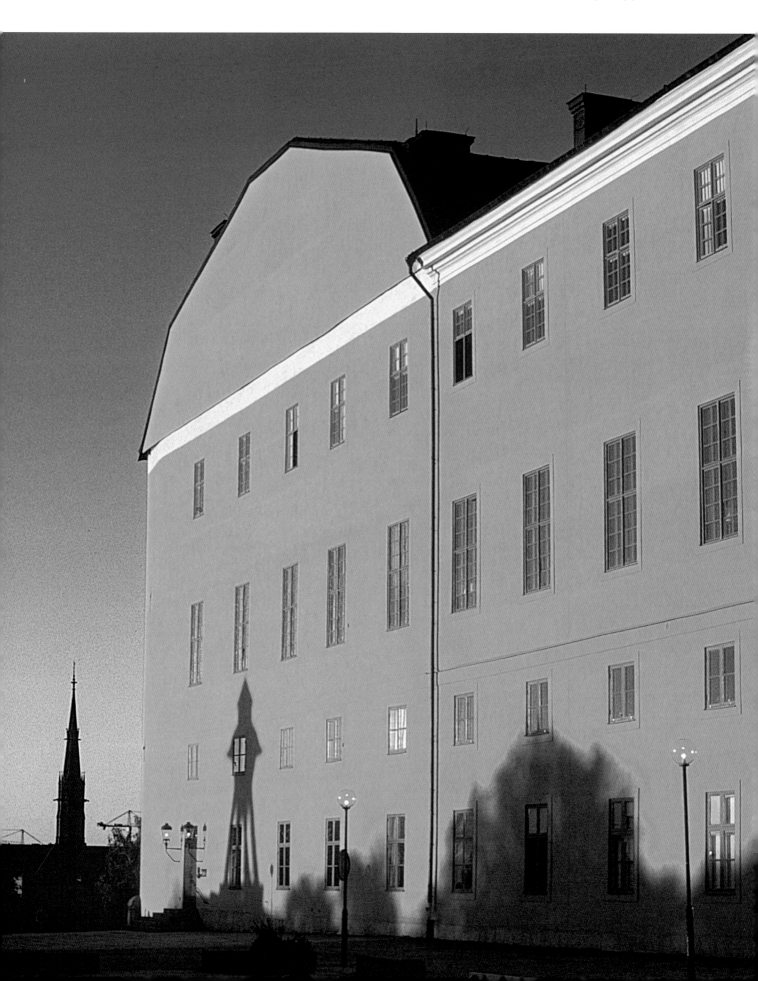

Tore Frängsmyr

The Great University

In 1477, Pope Sixtus IV decreed the establishment of Uppsala University. Thus, the institution was a church establishment. Archbishop Jacob Ulfsson initiated the effort and was named as the first chancellor. Highly educated canons commenced teaching the same year in the cathedral chapter. The Church not only needed trained priests, but also judicial personnel to administrate the Church's business.

Activities at the university quieted down after Jacob Ulfsson retired in 1515. During the Reformation initiated by Gustaf Vasa in the 1520s, the university was placed on a back-burner because of lack of time, money and interest. Gustaf Vasa's sons made a gallant attempt to revive activities but in effect, the university was only a name until 1593. In that year, the "Uppsala Conclave" decided to breathe life into the University again. The primary reason for the revival was to avoid exporting students to other countries and thereby avoiding the influence of Catholicism.

Among the items which Gustaf II Adolf bequeathed to the University was the University House. The old school building, Academica Carolina, was still available but impractical. The new building, eventually called Gustavianum after the benefactor, was built across from the cathedral. Between 1622–25, a new building was

Gustavianum

erected under the supervision of the Dutch builder, Casper Panten.

Gustavianum housed almost the entire University operations. There were large halls for business pertaining to a university court, teaching halls, library, administration and a kitchen and dining room for the student community. There were also 26 rooms for students in the attic. Lectures and defence of theses continued to be conducted in the old Academia. Up until the mid-1800s Gustavianum was the main building of the University. A new University Library was built and this was followed by a new University house towards the end of the century.

Since then, Gustavianum has been used to house institutions and for lecture halls. In June 1997, the new University museum was opened, Museum Gustavianum.

Officially he was a professor of medicine, but he was a Renaissance man, and master of most trades. When 20 he discovered the lymphatic system and wrote his thesis on the circulation system. He planned and executed magnificent gardens, built bridges, waterways and locks, conducted archeological diggings and wrote historical works. Rudbeck wanted to draw all of the known plants in magnificent illustrations in his book *Campus Elysii*. He recruited his family, two daughters and his son, Olof the Younger who followed him as a professor. The greater part of the legacy was destroyed in the 1702 fire.

Rudbeck died only a few months

The University benefited during the time when Sweden acted as a major power in Europe. Sweden needed to live up to the levels maintained by the other power blocks on the European stage and this included the quality of higher education. During the 1620s, Gustaf II Adolf donated the money to build the Gustavianum and 300 freehold farms from his own inheritance. The rents and returns on the farms provided enough income for the University to be self-standing up until the 1830s. The University received a new charter and a highly-regarded chancellor, John Skytte.

The Anatomical Theatre

For a 17th century doctor, it was vital to have access to both a botanical garden and an anatomical theatre. When Olof Rudbeck returned from his fact-finding trip to Holland in the mid-1650s, he founded his first garden, now the Linné Garden. Then he tackled the problem of the anatomical theatre. He built a large magnificent cupola on Gustavianum's roof complete with a sun dial on the outside.

The new hall was called a theatre because the structure was designed so observers would be able to see from all vantage points. The forms could vary. Rudbeck chose the amphitheatre, with a rounded form, which had also been done earlier. On the other hand, his was unique in that it was built on the roof of a building. The room was designed in classic style with imitation wooden pillars. In the middle was the operating table with room for 200 observers.

Eventhough Rudbeck was an anatomist, there were few dissections carried out on human bodies; it was difficult to obtain bodies though suicide cases could be recruited. In lieu of human bodies, dogs or cats were used.

That the room can be compared to a temple is not an accident. Anatomical demonstrations were meant not only to reveal the inner workings and secrets of the human body but also give homage to the Creator's power and ingenuity. This is why the general public was invited to witness dissections, which also became a favourite entertainment.

The theatre was torn down during the 1800s but re-built during the 1950s after Rudbeck's plans.

Tore Frängsmyr

Recruitment of new teachers reached into the rest of Europe and particularly in Germany. Soon the University was on a par with other European universities. In the 1660s, a feud broke out between Olof Rudbeck and his colleagues on the one side and the theologians. The 35-year long battle concerned Rudbeck's drive to introduce Descartes' philosophy in the University and only ended when the king forbade further discussions of the issue.

During the 1700s, the scientific revolution made headway with support from the political structure. The politicians viewed science as a motor to spur Sweden's economy after the disastrous wars of the King, Carl XII. Within about 50 years (about 1735–85), Swedish scientists from Uppsala became world-leaders in their fields. The botanist Carl von Linné revolutionised botany with his scientifically-based system of classification. Other names include Anders Celsius in astronomy, Samuel Klingenstierna in physics, J.G. Wallerius and Torbern Bergman in chemistry, Nils Rosén von Rosenstein in medicine (a pioneer in paediatrics) and more.

During the 1880s, the University was influenced by German Romanticism. The philosophy of idealism influenced the humanists, scientists and medical men. Several well-known professors included the historian Erik Gustaf Geijer, the physician Israel Hwasser and the philosopher Christopher Jacob Boström. Critics of the university maintained that the institution muddled by with outdated teachings and should be moved to Stockholm, the centre of finance and trade. The discussions continued for almost 50 years, but the University remained in Uppsala. During the second half of the 1800s, the physical sciences blossomed with a number of well-regarded researchers with Anders Ångström at the forefront.

In this panorama we see a familiar profile of central Uppsala. On the right is Värmland's Nation, designed by Ragnar Östberg and completed in 1930. This is one of the most elegant nation buildings in Uppsala. Next is the Oxenstierna house

Riddartorget

which housed the first University Hospital with six beds at the beginning of the 1800's. It now houses the faculty of law and is called Juridicum.

Immediately in front is Skytteanum, which houses the holder of the Skytteanum chair of political science and the institution of political science. The house was donated to the University by John Skytte in 1662 during the same year he was named chancellor. Skytte was an erudite humanist and clever civil servant; he was Gustaf II Adolf's teacher and closest advisor

The chair retains its requirements for the holder to excel in "eloquence and political science."

Throughout the 20th century, Uppsala University has maintained its national and international reputation as an educational institution. Cutting-edge researchers founded schools including the philosophers Axel Hägerström and Adolf Phalén, the literature historian Henrik Schück, and the Asian Studies expert H.S. Nyberg. Advances in sciences were made by Nobel Prize winners Kai Siegbahn in physics, The Svedberg in physical chemistry and Arne Tiselius in biochemistry. The original four faculties have grown and divided to the present seven faculties. About 30 000 students are involved in the University's programs. Of the almost 5 000 employees, about 2 000 are researchers and teachers.

One of the most famous figures during the early 1900s was Henrik Schück (1855–1947), professor in comparative literature between 1898 until 1920. In addition, he was vice chancellor between 1905–18. He was an unbelievably prolific author and published among other things extensive works in comparative literature in several volumes. In 1913 he was elected to the Swedish Academy. After retirement, he moved to Stockholm where he was also chairman of the Nobel Foundation between 1918–29.

The portrait which hangs in the vice-chancellor's room was painted by Anders Zorn in 1915 and shows Schück in formal dress with the emblem of the North Star Order and the Chancellor's chain.

The Main University Building

During the 1877 celebrations of the University's 400th jubilee, plans were laid for a new University building. A stipend from the state was granted but because of a long, drawn out contest among architects for the best plans plus other problems, it was not until the spring of 1879 that King Oscar II could lay the cornerstone.

The University Main Building was built on the hill above Gustavianum on the site which once was Rudbeck's old stable. The building is recorded as one of the prime examples of Swedish monumental architecture from the end of the 19th century. The pompous hall has a beautifully decorated ceiling and three cupolas. There is a seating area for 2 000 people. Offices for the university board and the chancellor's officer occupy the first floor. On the next floor there are more offices for the various faculties which still are used as meeting rooms. In

the middle there is a Chancellor's room where portraits of previous chancellors hang.

The new University building contained 11 lecture halls which represented a great step forward both for the lecturers and students.

Earlier, only a few, unheated rooms were available in Gustavianum. A number of critical voices thought the new building was much too luxurious and that it gave the wrong impression to the students. However, even today, the building is used effectively.

Students also received a monumental warning before entering the building. During the time the house was built, discussions were held about free love at the student organisation Verdandi. This was so shocking that the professors decided that an inscription over the entrance to the new aula would be the citation from the poet Thomas Thorild "Free thinking is great, right thinking is greater."

In the University Park in front of the University Main Building, there is a statue of Erik Gustaf Geijer. As a poet, historian and composer, he was one of the famous names from Uppsala University from the 19th century. The statue was made by John Börjeson and was unveiled in October, 1888.

Tore Frängsmyr

The Road of Knowledge

In the beginning, one building was enough to house the University. Eventually, growth created a need for more space. Now the University is spread throughout the city. In the United States, a university area is usually termed a campus because a large area had been set aside for buildings and expansion. In Uppsala, growth has occurred in bouts and spurts for nearly 500 years while reflecting the organic growth of the city. Most of the oldest buildings are in the centre of town. On the perimeters of town there are larger, more modern areas which could possibly be referred to as a campus.

Cathedral School graced Riddartorget for 400 years. After the fire of 1702, the school wandered about until it arrived at its present address in 1869.

A starting point could be Cathedral School, which traces its roots to the Middle Ages. All diocesan capitals had their own schools for religious training and thus Cathedral School is one of the oldest. The address has changed several times. The school now on Skolgatan was ready for occupancy in 1869 and additions have been added since then.

Kitty-corner from Cathedral School is the University's building baptised as Ekonomikum because of the intellectual pursuits contained within its walls. This elongated building stretches its way along Kyrkogårdsgatan to the farthest corner of the University's most northern point of the campus along the "Road of Knowledge".

Ekonomikum was designed by Peter Celsing and opened in 1975.

Tore Frängsmyr

The Aula

In the centre of the University
Main Building is the Aula, a
large assembly hall, with a
beautiful ceiling and a large
cupola. The University's
celebrations and ceremonies
are held here. At the end of
every Spring term, conferment
of doctor's degrees takes place
for all who have completed
their doctoral work during
the year. The new doctors
receive symbols of rank; a
diploma, a ring and a doctor's
hat (or a wreath of bay leaves
for those in the humanities).
Other ceremonies also take
place such as the installation
of new professors who hold
their addresses and are
introduced into their new
roles by the Rector
Magnificus, the title of the
University president. Other
activities in the Aula include
concerts, performing arts
programs, large conferences
and lectures.

Oases of Knowledge

There are scholarly environments pricking the landscape surrounding the Cathedral and the University. In front of the Cathedral in St. Erik's Square you can see the old house of the university council which was designed by Carl Hårleman in the middle of the 1700s. This is just one of the buildings used by Ingmar Bergman in his film *Fanny and Alexander*. For many years the building housed the Art Institute and later archaeological subjects. To the right of the old university board's building and in front of Gustavianum you can see the Ekerman's house built by Petrus Ekerman, professor of Latin, in 1761. This housed the History Institute and was called Historicum. Next is the Royal Society of Sciences. This building houses Sweden's oldest scientific academy started in 1710 as a little group called "Collegium curiosorum" (Thirst for Knowledge Guild). In 1719, it became the Bokwetts-Gillet and ended up in 1728 as the Royal Society of Sciences. The Schefferus library in the garden is a little stone structure from the 1660s possibly designed by Olof Rudbeck. The books had to be kept in a stone house to avoid risk of fire. Schefferus was a learned language professor from Strasbourg who authored a book on Lappland (*Lapponia*, 1673).

Royal Society of Sciences is on St. Erik's Square. In the shadows under the great tree is the Schefferus library.

Carolina Rediviva

The University Library had been housed in Gustavianum since the 1620s. However, lack of space soon forced plans for a new library. Plans made during Gustaf III's time were

The University Library, Carolina Rediviva is on the high throne of Drottninggatan.

never realised. A number of locations were discussed. When Carl Johan as the University Chancellor visited in 1811, the question of a new location was revived. The Crown prince pointed to the brow of a hill with Drottninggatan stating it would be appropriate at that place. And so it was.

The royal manager Carl Fredrik Sundvall was commissioned to draw up plans for the library. It took time. The building began in 1820 but it met with delays and high costs. It was in 1841 that the new library could be opened. At this point over 100 000 volumes had been moved from Gustavianum.

The new library had glorious, large rooms. On the top floor, a party room was created called Carolina hall. Banquets, balls and other celebrations were held here including the Scandinavist meetings. It was here that the choir "Allmänna Sången" first performed the famous step march with "Viking home, aged groves ..."

A banquet room with lighted candles was hardly an appropriate addition to a library. Eventually, the celebrations were moved to the University Main Building and the Aula. In addition, space was needed for the large book collection. New floors were put in to divide Carolina Hall and it was changed into a storage area for books. Since then, the area has been added to on several occasions including the construction of a subterranean depository. The latest addition was during the 1960s with Peter Celsing as architect.

Below the castle and neighbour to Carolina Rediviva is Geijer's garden.

When the new university library was opened, the oldest university building had been removed, Academia Carolina. In remembrance, the new building was called Carolina Rediviva, or the "resurrected Carolina".

Tore Frängsmyr

Kemikum and Fysikum

Since the middle of the 19th century, scientists have gathered at Thunbergsvägen across the street from the Botanical garden. Gamla (Old) Chemicum from 1859 housed the chemists but also the physicists. The building has later been renamed after its shifting tenants from Philosophicum, Philogicum, Mathematicum etc. Now the historians and theologians are residents. The chemists built a new institution, Kemikum, which was ready in 1904. Since then, buildings have been added. Fysikum was built immediately behind this in 1908. Much later in the 1960s, Teknikum was built along Villavägen.

During the 1990s, the Mathematics Department moved to a locale which had belonged to the army around Polacksbacken. Physics and technology students together with some chemists have moved to the new Ångström Laboratory while other chemists will have BMC as their address. This area together with the English Park and Carolina Rediviva will be the cornerstones of a Humanities campus.

Kemikum and Fysikum became the Humanities campus.

Akademiska sjukhuset
(The Academic Hospital)

Alvar Gullstrand (1862–1930), was Uppsala's first professor of ophtalmiatrics (eye disease) in 1894 after writing his dissertation on astigmatism. Being a whiz at mathematics, he used his gift to calculate optic lenses and refraction. He coined the term dioptre as a measure of lens strength. Gullstrand contributed to making many instruments for investigations of the eye. In 1911 he was awarded the Nobel Prize for his work. As a tribute to Gullstrand, the photographer raises his own glasses in front of the eye clinic.

The first Academic hospital, Nosocomium Academicum, was located in the Oxenstierna House in 1708 (now Juridicum) complete with six beds. Rest and a curative environment could be difficult at times because there was a pub located in the same building. The first modern hospital was built in 1867 and has undergone additions and new construction making it almost a city within itself. The area is bordered by Dag Hammarskjöld's Väg on the west, and Sjukhusvägen to the south and east. The Hospital is both a teaching hospital and serves the region with about 1 500 patients cared for by 8 000 employees.

Akademiska sjukhuset (the Academic Hospital).

Tore Frängsmyr

Botanical Garden

The Botanical Garden, also designed by Rudbeck the Elder, belonged to the castle until Gustaf III Adolf bequeathed it to the University. Louis Jean Desprez, Gustaf's architect, was commissioned to design a building for the grounds. However, completion took a long time. When it was finished in 1807, it was possible to honour Linné on the event of the 100-year jubilee of his birth by naming the building after him, Linneanum. Behind the columns in the middle there is an impressive hall named Linnéhallen. The Botanical Institution housed here continues the traditions.

A view from the Castle to the Baroque-style garden.

Evolutionary Biology Centre (EBC)

Next pages:
*A water garden with
tropical water lilies
occupies a section of
the green house.*

After several years of remodelling and rebuilding, the area
around the old Zoology and Paleonteology buildings have
reappeared with a new design, form and function, the
Evolutionary Biology Centre. In the buildings surrounding
the grassy quadrant, Uppsala's biologists gather to pursue
research in programmes as diverse as molecular evolution,
classification of plants, animal ecology, ecological toxico-
logy and population biology.

Genetics and study of the evolutionary origins of orga-
nisms' attributes give research its main thrust.

At EBC, you can see all sorts of things in the museums
from wonderful birds to fossils of dinosaurs. The
museums are open to the public.

The Evolutionary Biology Centre.

Tore Frängsmyr

Carl von Linné

One of the names Uppsala is most proud of is Carl von Linné (1707–78). Linné was a medical man which in the 18th century meant he was also a botanist. The Linné Garden was designed by Olof Rudbeck the Elder in the 1650s but was neglected until Linné came on the scene in 1728. Once Linné became a professor, he worked energetically with the architect Carl Hårleman to redesign the garden. Linné moved his household into the prefect's house built in the 1690s. The house is now a museum. He organised a greenhouse for his tropical plants. In 1735, Linné published *Systema naturae*, the Bible of plant classification, and became internationally recognised. His many

Linné Garden.

Statue of Carl von Linné sculpted by Carl Eldh.

botanical works were authored in Latin. His travel books about the Swedish landscape were written in the native language.

In 1758, Linné bought property in Hammarby and Sävja, just south of Uppsala. The main house is in Hammarby where he lived with his family during the summers. He gardened prolifically and often welcomed students and botanists to his home during the summers which is the best season for botanists.

His summer residence, Linné's Hammarby, is a few km south of Uppsala.

Polacksbacken (Polish Hill)

The Army had its training fields in area near Polacksbacken (Polish Hill), south of the Hospital. The wide fields offered housing plus room for military manoeuvres for Uppsala's regiment dating from 1680. In 1912, barracks were built for the infantry (I 8) and since the 1950s, the signal regiment (S 1) was housed there. Since the beginning of the 1990s, Uppsala University has moved mathematics and computer technique faculties to the area. Now it is a Mathematics and Information technology Centre (MIC). The officer training school was also located here between 1928–83. The area has become Uppsala Science Park with research and entrepreneurial firms as tenants.

On Polacksbacken, along the edge of the woods on the south, is the newest addition to the large institutional structures, Ångström Laboratory. The large interconnected buildings contain a number of University institutions in physics as well as inorganic chemistry and material sciences.

No one knows where the name "Polish Hill" came from but it is thought that Poles have something to do with it. One theory is that Sigismund's crowning in Uppsala in 1594 may have been the occasion for the label.

Anders Ångström (1814–74) was first an astronomer and later a professor in physics at Uppsala University (1858–74). He is considered to be one of the pioneers laying the grounds for spectroscopy. He conducted detailed studies of the sun's spectrum, *Aurora Borealis*, thermal conduction, and terrestrial magnetism.

The unit of measure Ångström (Å) is named after him and has been used for the tiniest atomic particles and wavelengths in spectroscopy.

His son also became a physics professor between 1896–1910.

The Ångström Laboratory in the upper part of the photograph houses institutions for chemistry, physics, material sciences and technology.

The old S 1. The university's mathematics and information technology centre is here.

Tore Frängsmyr

Biomedicinskt centrum – BMC
(Biomedical Centre)

On the other side of Dag Hammarskjöld's
Väg, a bit south of the hospital is the
Biomedical Centre composed of about 12
buildings. It was begun during the 1960s
and was finished in 1984. There are about
30 institutions including pharmacy, medicine,
life sciences from Uppsala University and the
Veterinary Medicine faculty from the
Swedish University of Agricultural Sciences.
There are about 1 000 employees and 1 500
students passing through here every year.

Biomedical Centre (BMC)

*Bror Marklund created the DNA helix
which has adorned BMC since 1977.*

Anders Celsius (1704–44) belonged to a famous family of mathematicians. Both his father and grandfather preceeded him in his professorial position awarded in 1730. Celsius took a long study trip throughout Europe and upon his return participated in a French geographical expedition to Torneå in northern Sweden during the winter 1736–37. He helped raise an observatory in a building on Svartbäcksgatan, which is still standing but has other uses.

Celsius was most famous for his 100-degree thermometer even though it had a freezing point at 100 and a boiling point at 0. Later, degrees on the thermometer were reversed.

Torbern Bergman (1735–84) was the second professor of chemistry in Sweden appointed in 1767. In his time, he was regarded as a prominent chemist and through countless experiments researched reactions of different substances in combination. The tendency of a substance to react he called affinity and noted his results in long affinity tables.

He examined spa waters and discovered that the waters contained carbonic acid, and thereafter could create artificial mineral water. In this way he is said to be the inventor of the modern soft drinks.

Carl Wilhelm Scheele (1742–86) was born in Stralsund, Germany which at that time belonged to Sweden, and came to Uppsala in 1770 after first being a chemist's apprentice in Göteborg, Malmö and Stockholm. He arrived at the Uplands Wapen, a chemist's located at Stora Torget where the department store Åhlen's is now located. He was a clever experimenter and developed a close collaboration with Torbern Bergman. From 1775, he was manager of a chemist shop in Köping.

Scheele is most famous for his discovery of oxygen which he called fire-air. In fact, he discovered oxygen before the Englishman Joseph Priestley. However, publication of his discovery was delayed and Priestly published his results first in 1774.

The Svedberg (1884–1971) became professor in physical chemistry in 1912 when he was only 28 years old.

He invented the ultracentrifuge and with the new instrument discovered that proteins are well defined molecules.

Svedberg's finding in the end created the new field of molecular biology, and his institution became internationally famous.

He organised and directed the Gustaf Werner Institute (1949–67) which has now been replaced by the The Svedberg Laboratory.

The Svedberg, whose real name was Theodor, was awarded the Nobel Prize in Chemistry in 1926.

Arne Tiselius (1902–71), professor in Biochemistry in 1938, was a student of The Svedberg but soon developed his own special area. He became an internationally recognised leader in his field.

Tiselius was given his own institution for biochemistry in 1946. He won the Nobel Prize for chemistry in 1948. Among his many contributions can be named that he was the first chairman of the Natural Science Research Council (1944–50) and was chairman of the Nobel Foundation (1960–64).

Kai Siegbahn, born in 1928, became professor in physics in 1954. His work in electron spectroscopy (ESCA) won him the Nobel Prize in physics in 1981. His father, Manne Siegbahn was also professor (1922–37) and was awarded the 1924 Nobel Prize in physics (received in 1925).

Tore Frängsmyr

The Swedish University of Agricultural Sciences

The same year that Uppsala University celebrated its 500-year jubilee a new university was founded in Uppsala, the Swedish University of Agricultural Sciences. The Forestry- and College of Veterinary Medicine moved from Stockholm to Uppsala to join the College of Agriculture at Ultuna. This is the only Agricultural University in Sweden.

Ultuna is located just south of Uppsala on an impressive and beautiful campus. The name Ultuna comes from the old Norse god, Ull. Since the time of Gustaf Vasa, the area was a crown property, which was redesigned during the 1600s as a royal barn to house livestock belonging to the household of the county governor living at Uppsala Castle. During the 1840s, an agricultural institute was founded to educate and train professions within the agricultural sector. In the 1930s this was reorganised into the College of Agriculture.

Research and teaching are carried out in about 50 areas in agriculture, horticulture, environmental sciences, forestry, water resources, veterinary medicine and food science.

The veterinarians are part of the Swedish University of Agricultural Sciences.

Growing near the Centre for Genetics is an avenue arched with birches. The most northerly trees were taken from the most northern part of Sweden. Those in the southern portion were rooted in the south of Sweden and then planted here. The trees prepare for the winter with the first warnings of autumn. By mid-September, the northern trees begin to shed their leaves. The southern imports remain a luscious green several weeks longer.

The spring brings about waves of green starting at the southern tip of the avenue.

The Avenue illustrates that the plants that are genetically adapted to a predetermined seasonal pattern remain true to the pattern even after changing environment.

Tore Frängsmyr

Research covers the different aspects of man in relation to use of natural resources. In this respect, the practical questions about environmental problems and relations between biology and technique are the basic starting points. Some research stations are located in other places such as Alnarp, Skara and Umeå.

Degrees are offered in agronomy, horticulture, landscape architecture, forestry and veterinary medicine. Other courses train students to be agricultural foremen or forest managers. The average number of students is 2 500. About 3 500 people including 150 professors are busy at the campus.

Sweden's largest veterinary hospital, the National Veterinary Institute, is located near Ultuna's campus. Here you can often see nervous masters and mistresses sitting in the waiting room with ailing house pets.

Contagious disease control is also carried out here in close collaboration with the Veterinary Medicine faculty.

In the Garden of Knowledge, important problems are demonstrated in a simple and clear way. The curious can learn about plants, biodiversity, farming systems and methods of tillage. The research is carried out under the auspices of the Swedish University of Agricultural Sciences and is presented in the form of small scale demonstration plots or as information signboards. Some of the areas include:

\# *field weeds from by-gone days*
\# *green mulch crops in organic farming*
\# *crop rotation*
\# *plant protection*

Mankind has been busy with improving animals and plants since the first settling for about 15 000 years ago. Then, as now, the goal was to refine the attributes such as yields and hardiness. Included among the traditional techniques are crossbreeding, but also spontaneous eruption of mutations that are preserved through selection. Crossbreeding allows transferring of attributes between closely related species. If attributes to be introduced are not found in closely-related species, newer techniques must be used , such as transferring specific genes (transformation).

With modern breeding techniques it is possible to change a plant's cultivation characteristics. Examples of this include plants that are resistant to damaging insects, to herbicides, and plants with increased tolerance for cold and frost. Even plants' nutritional needs can be changed. One example is "Golden rice", rice with a raised level of the vitamin A-precursor betacarotene. Vitamin A deficiency causes over one million deaths in the Third World annually and results in blindness in more than 300 000 children.

Tore Frängsmyr

Students and student life

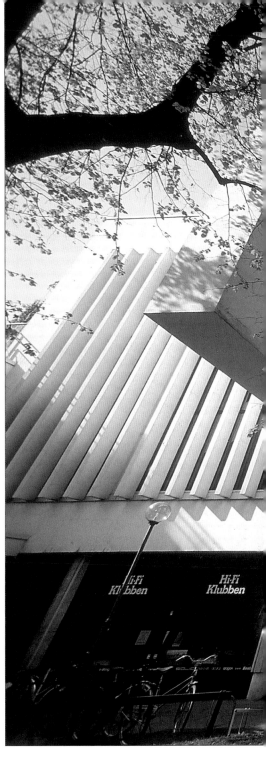

The first students in Uppsala in all likelihood lived communally in a sort of a common lodging house on the little mill islet jutting out in the Fyris River, now the site of the Museum of Uppland. That's why the area is called the Student's islet. During the 1600s, a royal stipend program was developed but that was only available to a few students. Most students were privately lodged and many had their food bags supposed to last the whole term with them from home. Sometimes students were forced to take leave from their studies to earn money as tutors.

In the middle of the 1600s, a new institution came into being known as the nations. This was a sort of friendship fraternity based on the geographical origins of the students. Students from the same province or town joined in each fraternity. The term nation originated from the division into nations which had taken place at the University of Paris. Even in the 1700s most students came from homes of the clergy. In the mid-1700s, there were about 1 000

Västgöta nation faces the Fyris River.

Västmanland-Dala nation is located in a building designed by the Finnish architect, Alvar Aalto and completed in 1965.

students. However, this number fell at the end of the century. By 1780, there were less than 400 students.

The 1800s were the fat years for students. The growing middle-class more and more sought education for their children. Students could be identified as a special group within the society. They instituted their own traditions and a number of the larger "nations" constructed their own houses. A student council was formed and students became active participants in cultural life. National songs

On-going research.

Lecture at B[

were sung, students demonstrated when Carl XIV Johan visited Uppsala. Scandinavianism became a voluntary political movement in which students from both Uppsala and Lund's University in southern Sweden played leading roles. The white student caps were used for the first time in 1843 in Uppsala and soon became a symbol of being a student. Uppsala was called "the city of perpetual youth" after the perpetual student and poet, Johan Nybom. Students represented youth, happiness and optimism. By the mid-1800s, there were about 1 500 students.

Uppsala society fluttered around the famous poets Geijer and Atterbom. Literary salons became regular meeting places. The most famous salons were held by a widowed Colonel's wife Malla Silfverstolpe from 1820 till about 1860. Music and song were a part of the salon culture. Gunnar Wennerberg performed with *Gluntarne* (released 1849–51) which described the joy and problems of two students,

...any students prefer to study in the ...niversity Library's quiet study halls.

Glunten and Magistern. The famous choirs also came into being: the Allmänna sången choir began in 1830 and then the Orphei Drängar (OD) was begun in 1853.

Modern times exploded on the university campus during the 1960s. The number of students constantly increased and housing became a repeated problem.

Attic creep-holes or tiny lodging rooms no longer were acceptable. The "nations" began building quantities of housing though the student council was forced to erect temporary barracks to handle the crisis. Housing is still a huge problem at the beginning of every new term. The larger number of students in every class also created continuity in teaching. The large, public lectures were increasingly replaced by teaching in smaller groups.

1968 was a politically tumultuous year for students, though not as violent in Uppsala as in other places.

The Walpurgis Eve Rituals

1. The dawn begins with a **champagne breakfast** with porridge, preferably consumed along the Fyris River.
2. **Shooting the rapids** at 10 am. Armed with life vests and helmets, the brave venture forth in their floats completed in the previous night.
3. After recycling the float remains from the morning's endeavours, a **herring lunch** outside, weather permitting, or in the dormitory.
4. Next item is a walk to Castle hill for the **Cap Ceremony** in front of Carolina Rediviva together with about 70 000 other participants. At the stroke of 3 pm, the Rector Magnificus standing on the balcony, lifts his white cap and signals the welcome to Spring. All others follow suit and then walk down the hill.
5. **Champagne race** means the students go to the nations to drink champagne but more often to meet friends, dance out-of-doors, and generally be happy.
6. Many arrive at the **University Park** to listen via a sound system to the OD choir singing the traditional Spring songs at the University Aula.
7. Those still with energy go to the **parties at the nations**.
8. At 9 pm, it is time for the **Allmänna sången choir and the annual speech** given by the student body's vice president at the Gunilla bell tower in front of the castle.
9. The **long night** between April 30 and May 1 has begun.
10. Some may take a break and participate in the nations formal **May Banquet** on May 1.

The English park is a favourite place for herring lunch.

Next pages:
After the cap ceremony on Walpurgis Eve, students wander down Castle Hill.
Earlier the students were supposed to rush down the hill to obtain a good table at the City Hotel on the corner of Trädgårdsgatan. However, at the end of the 1960s, there were far too many students to allow this sort of sprinting ... to a hotel which had closed its doors.

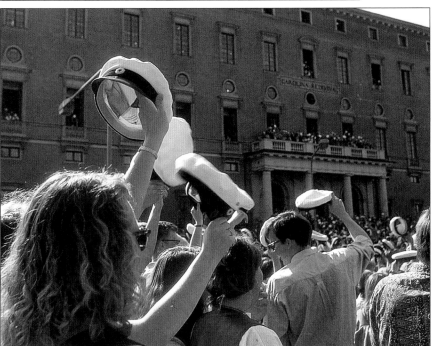

Cap ceremony on Castle Hill and champagne race in Värmland's Nation garden.

Old friends meet in the University Park listening to the OD choir singing traditional spring songs..

Tore Frängsmyr

Radical expression took its form in revolt and loud demonstrations. At the same time, many groups were campaigning for more international solidarity.

Today, student life is a mixture of the old and the new. The nations are active and now number 13. Membership is required of all students, even though there have been attempts to change this. There are still activities at the nations including celebrations of yearly events such as Walpurgis Eve on April 30, St. Martin's Day in November, and Lucia processions in December. In addition, the nations arrange a special celebration at the beginning of every term for new students who are called freshmen.

However, everything is not one, big party. Studies are also demanding and students must pass their exams to retain the student loan. Today there is no place for the perpetual students of the 1800s. The average student is certainly both more ambitious and hardworking.

STORK, *the student orchestra festival, is held in Uppsala every other year.*

Allmänna sången sings Spring songs and the student body's vice president delivers a speech at the Gunilla bell tower on Walpurgis Eve.

Where else but Uppsala could you meet lovely ladies in beautiful gowns on a sunny May morning? After the Spring Ball!

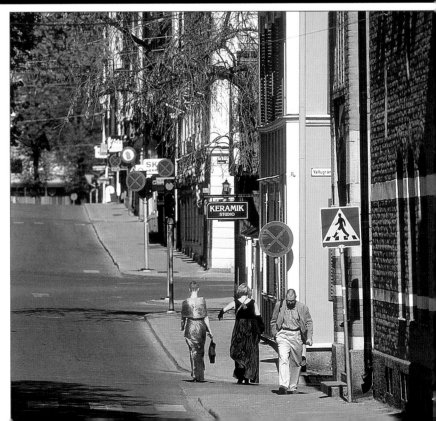

Profiles in Uppsala

Prince Gustaf

Oscar I's oldest son, Carl XV and the younger Gustaf came to Uppsala in 1844 to study. They lived in the Prince's House (Prinshuset) on Bäverns gränd near the steamboat harbour. Shortly after, their little brothers, Oscar II and August arrived. One generation later, Oscar's four sons moved into Prinshuset.

Gustaf (1827–52) was a music-loving prince and also duke of Uppland. He adapted well to Uppsala. His musical gifts blossomed in his contact with the literary salons and a willing though hard-to-please public and with the support and good advice from experienced composers like Lindblad and Geijer.

Many of Gustaf's melodies became classics among students and male choirs. Three of them are symbolically portrayed on the pillar of the graceful statue of Carl Eldh from 1927: these can be translated directly with "Sing of Students' Happy Days", "Happy as a Bird in the Morning", and "My Living Hours are Dwindling".

Prince Gustaf stands today between Carolina Rediviva and Geijer's garden. His profile is outlined against the Clason garden built in 1698 by Olof Rudbeck, later, during the 1800s the town's post-office, and now an international conference centre.

Gunnar Wennerberg

That the statue of the young Gunnar Wennerberg is placed on Carolina Hill surrounded by boisterous and musical students is more than appropriate. Wennerberg (1817–1901) stands as a symbol for the foot-loose-fancy-free student life of song, joyous celebration which precedes the advent of the middle-class drudgery of daily boredom loaded with 'musts'. In his collection *Gluntarne* (1849–51) both the students Glunten and Magistern sing duets about pubs, lectures, walks, loves, borrowed money, moonlight and exams, in such ways that the students from Uppsala even today recognise their own own pains and joys. "Uppsala is best" is the title of one of the songs.

The gist of the tune is that Uppsala is a wonderful place which tolerated bohemian behaviour while reserving judgement.

However, Glunten must leave the student town, and as Wennerberg himself, become successful careerist in service to society. Wennerberg was successful. He became an ecumenical minister, governor for the county, a member of the Order of the Seraphim, and, with time, rather devout.

Dag Hammarskjöld

Dag Hammarskjöld (1905–61) was the General Secretary of the UN from 1953 until he died in an airoplane crash while on a peace mission in Africa. Shortly thereafter, his diary filled with philosophical and mystical reflections, *Markings*, was published.

Dag replaced his father, Hjalmar in the Swedish Academy. His father had been the county governor and Dag grew up in the Castle. In Geijers garden, not far from the castle, is the centre bearing his name which has been dedicated to research and education on issues facing less-developed countries.

A little farther away is the family grave in the Old Graveyard.

Dag Hammarskjöld's great interest in nature followed the Linnéan tradition and is expressed in many ways from the mountains to the fields of Skåne but also in a little essay describing his childhood on Castle Hill:

The sky deepens as evening approaches. Instruments are put away and when the Gunilla bell tower signals 9, Castle Hill is once again alone. The early summer's silent escorts take over. The lilacs protect the hedgehogs in a loving embrace. The insects flock around the nuts on the whitebeam. For a few short hours, Castle Hill returns to its silent life as just one of many hills along the Uppsala Ridge.

Ingmar Bergman

Ingmar Bergman often stayed with his grandmother on Trädgårdsgatan as a child. In his autobiography *Laterna Magica (Magical Lanterns)* (1986), he describes his love for the underground of light, sounds and smells. Grandmother's flat was re-created in the film *Fanny and Alexander* (1982) which also used many other scenes from Uppsala. The early visits to Uppsala were important in Bergman's development as a film director. One of the nearby cinemas was Slotts, located in the Hantverksföreningens house. During the 1990s, the cinema was renovated and in tribute to Bergman is called *Laterna Magica*. It looks the same as it did when grandmother took the little boy to the cinema more than half a century ago.

She loved to go to the cinema, and if it was allowed for children (ratings on Monday mornings, page 3, in the local newspaper), she didn't wait until Saturday or Sunday afternoon. Only one thing marred our joy. Grandmother had a horrendous pair of galoshes and wasn't particularly fond of love scenes, which I, on the other hand, heartily enjoyed. When the hero and heroine languished and groped too long, grandmother's galoshes began squeaking. The teeth-grating noise reverberated throughout the theatre.

The actress Viveca Lindfors (1920–95) was born in the same building.

Carl Milles

High above the ridge called Kronåsen on the southern edge of town, Sten Sture the Elder and his band can be seen marching to the Battle at Brunkenberg in 1471. Carl Milles' statue was erected in 1925 after much commotion. "A lot of stone, but not much Sture" many thought. The double entendre in Swedish is that Sten translates as stone. As it is now, the statue can only be viewed from a distance; the best view is from the Uppsala Science Park area, where Uppsala's think tanks are located. Many have tried to bring Sten Sture back to the earth and place him more centrally. However, the inaccessibility of art for the public was part of Carl Milles program:

... to place a monument in a city is to destroy the idea. I have so many great ideas in my head that I pray to God I can carry out but all of them are planned for isolated locations, where they would appear as a bolt of lightning ...

Bror Hjorth

A grinning water-sprite with both instruments raised, the physical and the musical. An affirmation of love from a lady of the woods with open arms. Spinning dancers among sunflowers. Cascades of sprinkling water over the glittering bronze. Bror Hjorth's statue Näckens polska is the first thing train passengers meet when they come to Uppsala. And lust for life is awakened.

I have felt like a fiddler in wood, stone and clay with a fiddler's limitations but also with his experience of nature's wonder: great forests and roaring rapids.

Bror Hjorth's home near the Botanical Garden is now a homey museum giving the impression that the artist has only temporarily left his studio.

Kerstin Ekman

On the middle of the hill on St. Johannes Street is a tradition-laden cafè. "Päron" Lindblad, the main character in Kerstin Ekman's detective story, *Pukehornet* (1967), arrives after wandering from Petterslund through the centre of town to Övre Slottsgatan. He meets some friends with "transparent coffee in cups and the bottled drink with an extraordinary cork on the table."

He knew about the café. It was called Uroxen and had ugly murals on the walls. Mostly lorry drivers sat there and errand boys on their lunch break would trade gossip at the pinball machines.

The paintings, in naive style, are still there and contribute to the café's ambience. But, "Päron" was not receptive to its charms. He had a dead body to worry about.

Lars Gustafsson

Slöjdgatan on Kungsgärdet copies the old plan of a workers' community. The wooden houses painted in pastel tones give a small-town character to the area designed by the architect Gunnar Leche in the 1920s. The houses are now attractive one-family homes created from the earlier four-flat structures, which housed the workers from the nearby brick and tile factory, Uppsala-Ekeby. An early retiree, Torsten Bergman, named in Lars Gustafsson's novel, *En kakelsättares eftermiddag* (1991), was the author's neighbour when he lived there around 1980. One grey November day, Torsten awakens to a dreary workday:

The garden was ragged, the horizon askew. The house was old, at one time painted green, now peeling its grey-blue scales. Tired branches from heavy, old apple trees threatened the rotting porch. The garden was full of trash, a messy monument to the sum of his working life. And someone might say, his failure.

Christer Åsberg

Gösta Knutsson

Uppsala's most famous literary figure is the cat, Pelle Svanslös (tail-less) and his good, and lesser friends, who haunt the streets and cellars around Åsgränd, the block between the University and the graveyard. Their creator was Gösta Knutsson (1908–72). For several decades, he was in the limelight for Uppsala's cultural life. He organised radio programs and entertained the nation with a quiz program during the war years.

One can discover personality traits and reputations of many Uppsala characters in the dialogue of the cats in Knutsson's books. His understanding of human nature appears in his characters' symbolism.

Pelle Svanslös lived here with Maja Gräddnos.

Are any cats there?

The kind Pelle, the nasty Måns, the tiresome echoes of Bill and Bull, the charming Maja Gräddnos, the sweet Gullan from Arcadia, the farmer Murre from Skogstibble etc.

A popular entertainment for tourists is to wander the streets and alleys as Pelle once did. The guide takes one behind the fences, and through cellar windows, in drainpipes and mailboxes where it is possible to imagine the dizzy adventures the animal-lover Knutsson created for his cats.

If more exercise is desired by the female sex, it is possible to run in the Maja Gräddnos race which bursts forth every Ascension Thursday boasting about 15 000 participants of all ages, nationalities and modes of transportation including legs, wheelchairs, baby carriages and walkers.

Maja Gräddnos race.

Christer Åsberg

Owe Thörnqvist

Engelska parken (English park) behind Carolina Rediviva (University Library) was first planted in 1805 upon the initiative of the botanist C.P. Thunberg. An avenue of lindens graces the centre. The park is inviting for children seeking adventure and for the older, more staid visitors, boule and relaxing picnics. Earlier it attracted livelier visitors. In the middle of the 1800s, it was the scene for markets, games and dance. At the beginning of the 20th century, it was the gathering place for the agitators of the new social movements with their array of followers. Outside of Uppsala, it is best known in one of Owe Thörnqvist's breakthrough melodies:

We dance the rumba in Engelska parken
We plant a cactus in the ground
A little palm from a flower shop
We placed there in Engelska parken.

Thörnqvist immortalised many other places in Uppsala in his songs, "Gun from Dragarbrunn", "Svartbäckens Reddest Rose" and "There is a Sausage Man Down at Fyris Torg".

Christer Åsberg

The small town which grew

By the mid 1800s, Uppsala was a little town with about 10 000 residents. Educating bureaucrats, churchmen and administrators dominated the scene. The symbols for this were the university, cathedral and castle. A few paint factories and tanneries were located along the Fyris River and nearby were carpentry shops and workshops. After the 1850s, Uppsala was decorated with parks and showy homes of the wealthy. The railroad snaked through Uppsala — after a battle with the competing village of Örsundsbro. A municipal gasworks plant was built next to the expanding harbour, water systems were organised and sewage lines were built. The glacial clay deposited millennia ago created favourable conditions for the characteristic Uppsala industry, brick-making. Brick-makers surrounded the town in Luthagen, Vaksala, Librobäck and Uppsala-Ekeby. Other older industries which began about the same time include Uppsala Ångkvarn, now Nord Mills, Ättiksfabriken, now owned by the conglomerate Marabou, which launched its successful mustard product, Slottsenap in the 1920s, and Gahn's technique and chemical factory (which closed its doors in 1968).

At the turn of the century, the garment industry, shoes, printers and machines shops appeared on the scene. Bicycle production was especially associated with Uppsala. Nymans was the largest industry with Hermes and Crescent the most famous among the many quality trademarks which flourished here. By the 1950s, Uppsala was a leading industrial town, though nostalgia and a romantic view preferred to see the town as a student paradise. However, the era of industry also became a subject for nostalgia.

Next page:
At St. Johannesgatan in the Övre Slotts block.

Next pages:
Övre Slottsgatan and St. Johannesgatan intersection.

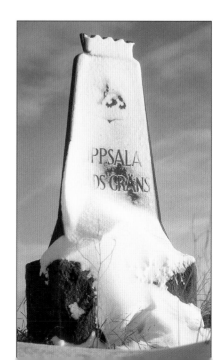

122

The old blocks around
Övre Slottsgatan.

Övre Slottsgatan (Upper Castle Road)

> *Old is this road*
> *Run-down these houses*
> *Old is the world*
> *Which was there before you.*
> (Lars Gustafsson, *Öfre Slottsgatan*)

Huge areas in the heart of Uppsala were torn down to make way for new office and merchandising complexes during the 1960s and '70s. The renewal frenzy found opposition which gathered under the banner, Preserve Uppsala, which sought to save the valuable city environment. The area around Övre Slottsgatan between the University House and Cathedral School survived the wrecking ball. Most of the façades have been faithfully restored. Together with the courtyards behind the façades, we get an idea of the way things were when only gaslights lighted the streets and Strindberg (author), Fröding (poet) and Albert Engström (author & humorist) lived here.

The old town

In the Middle Ages, long, small blocks stretched out to the east from the river. Every block was a type of farm. Any street names were only temporary. The first time a street was named was in 1231 when Our Blessed Lady's Church was given property 'between those roads which ran on either side and continued to the ditch with the field.' St. Per's Church was also on the east side and a Franciscan cloister, whose walls are now laid bare. After a fire in 1543, the bricks from the church were used to build Gustaf Vasa's castle.

Here and there can be seen traces of the old town. The public well, Dragarbrunn, is commemorated in the street. The name may come from a shortening of the Dragarbro-gatsbrunn, after a street which was arch-shaped going to the ferry on the river above the Mill Falls. In the intersecting road is the observatory built by Anders Celsius in 1738. It was erected on top of an older house and because it was recessed from the road, it was not demolished in the new building plan during the 1600s and also stands as an example of how property was divided in the Middle Ages.

The east side of Stora Torget (Central Square).

The Celsius building and ruins of the cloister hint at the original street plan of the city.

128

Stora Torget (central square)

Stora Torget's west side.

There are several shopping plazas in the town centre.

The city plan of 1643 called for making the centre of town into a rectangle, 800 x 1200 m, with straight-as-arrow roads, boxed in by the city wall. The underlying plan can still be seen today. A large central square was planned as the meeting point for the four roads leading to the centre. The large buildings tightly packed together reinforce the square's form. Rådhuset (town hall) completed in 1883 and Uplands Bank from 1906 contribute to the countenance of official-dom. The Tempo department store from 1960 with its Moorish-inspired cement adornments created a travesty of the square's environment which residents have still not recovered from. To the west is the old Strandberg's textile building from the turn of the century and Skandia's building complex from 1963 adding its varying architectural expressions to the square's intended dignity.

Stora Torget is now more a bus stop than a meeting place. People meet in the shopping plazas that have repla-ced the department stores. But on the perimeter of town, the huge supermarkets, ICA, IKEA, coop Forum bait their traps. The competition between the shops in the centre of town and supermarkets is tough.

129

Vaksala torg

It took a long time for Uppsala to reach out to the east. The "Town Ditch", now Kungsgatan, was the boundary. By the 1860s, the railroad had expanded the town. At the turn of the century, farther out along Vaksala road, at old wind mill hill, a new torg (square) was built. Industries such as Nymans, Valskvarnen and Mejeriet, and residential areas such as Port Arthur and Tripolis, named after scenes of war battles, were showy strongholds surrounding it. Vaksala torg became the sight of the annual winter Distings market dating back to the Middle Ages. Farmers from all over came to the October market and to the market days once monthly. Now the torg is famous as a lively international meeting place. The May 1 parades and demonstrations either begin or end at Vaksala torg. In the summer, the old steam train, "Lenna-katten" embarks on a narrow-gauge rail from the nearby Östra Station chugging to Fjällnora, the joint summer spot of Uppsala's residents.

Vaksala torg was completed in 1927 when the monumental Vaksala school, designed by Uppsala's foremost architect, Gunnar Leche, stood in place. The building was the first of Anders Diös who went on to build many more in Uppsala. The schoolyard is a "torg" onto itself and several outlying squares create the thickly foliaged yards in the next blocks.

Christer Åsberg

The new Uppsala residents

Roughly 15 percent of Uppsala's residents now have foreign backgrounds, which amounts to about 25 000 people. This means that persons with foreign background are as many as the entire Uppsala population 75 years ago. Then, incidently, there were 73 foreign citizens living in Uppsala.

The first permanent foreign inroad in Uppsala would be the construction workers who laboured on the cathedral during the 1300s. In later phases, the university has attracted foreign teachers and specialists of different types. During the Second World War, there were many Norwegian students, and following the war, Uppsala received its part of the refugee waves from the Baltic states and Hungary. During the 1970s many refugees fled military dictatorships in Greece, Chile, and Argentina. Most of them adapted well and many have been able to return when the conditions in their homelands improved.

Since the 1980s, Uppsala has been something of a centre for Kurdish immigration. The Kurdish nationalist author, Cegerxwin, lived here during the last years of his life before he died in 1984. The most dramatic untoward events in the foreigners' Uppsala have been tied to the Kurdish

group. A defector from the extremist organisation, PKK, was murdered on Stora torget in 1984, and a liberated Kurdish girl, Fadime Sahindal, was killed by her father in what has been called an honour killing in 2002. During the 1990s, refugees have arrived from a number of lands including the former Yugoslavia and Iran.

Again, it is the university with its educational possibilities that attracts. This is not only true for refugees from different dictatorships, but it is also students and researchers from other countries. Still, it is most often that one meets the new Uppsala residents in service professions of one type or another. This can be a reason to say that Uppsala would come to a standstill if one, for a moment, dreamed away all of the foreigners who drive taxis in Uppsala, all of those who keep the small shops open at all hours of the day and night, or fill all of the vacancies in home service and care for the elderly.

At a well-received ceremony at the castle and in Odinslund during the national holiday on June 6, the City of Uppsala welcomes all those who have become Swedish citizens during the previous year.

The many waves of immigrants during the last half-century have enriched the city in many ways, including religiously. The Catholic Church has been in Uppsala since the 1930s but has grown markedly in recent years. There is a lively orthodox church in what was earlier a mission chapel. A Jewish congregation has been around a long time but it is small and does not have a formal synagogue. Since 1995, a mosque located in the Löten area towards Gamla Uppsala serves the large group of Muslims residents.

Christer Åsberg

The new city districts

From the end of the 1930s until about 1960, the population doubled. During the next 30 years, another doubling of the population to the present total of about 185 000 took place. Everyone has to live somewhere. Many residential buildings disappeared from town during this time.

New suburbs were built. An early example was Luthagen, which today is considered close to the town centre. A type of architectural determination and pre-determined social intercourse was the result of the well-planned areas built in the 1940s such as Tuna backar in the north and a bit later, Sala backar in the east. Eriksberg was built in the 1950s in a beautiful area filled with natural variations.

Stenhagen.

Gränby.

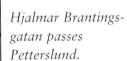

Hjalmar Brantings-gatan passes Petterslund.

The same was true for the independent city district of Gottsunda during the 1970s, Stenhagen during the 1980s and the 1990s Sävja. The wide-open landscape surrounding Uppsala was very inviting for the national program to provide housing for all, and the areas of Årsta, Gränby and Nyby sprang up. Suburban residential neighbourhoods such as Sunnersta, Bälinge, Vänge, Vilan and Storvreta have been added. Uppsala also absorbed some neighbouring counties.

Christer Åsberg

New industries

The large manufacturing industries were born of small craft enterprises. When they exited from the stage, they had laid the groundwork for the newer industries' intellectual capital in the high-tech area. When Pharmacia came to Uppsala in 1951, it found not only a university, but also a tradition in industrial chemistry and technology.

One branch of GE Health Care was Scanditronix with its precision instruments which is a follower to the mechanical workshops. Almqvist & Wiksell represented the printing industry for many years, and had successors in varying shapes from Scandecor as a global industry, to graphic artists and layout specialists working in small companies using technology made accessible by computer industries.

Pharmacia, now split and fusioned with foreign companies (Pfizer, Fresenius Kabi, GE Health Care), became the most important industry when most traditional manufacturing disappeared during the 1960s–70s.

The pharmaceutical industry was an early example of the co-operation between industry and universities on basic research. This has been and must be a constant for Uppsala with its two universities. In recent years a number of smaller companies (biggest is Q-Med) have been created on basis of exciting innovations, often in biotechnology.

Neither the centuries of tradition nor the present-day proven competence can compete with the next century's demands for development tools and flexibility.

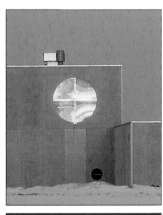
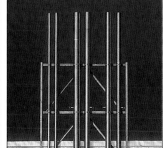

Bird's-eye view of Uppsala Science Park.

The sculpture, To the Horse, *created by Lennart Huck Hultgren at the entrance to Uppsala Science Park is a reminder of the bygone days of the military.*

Uppsala Science Park

For a long time, Uppsala was an important military outpost. Both the infantry and artillery regiments were quartered around Polacksbacken to the south of town. The military presided over the Army Officer School and teacher training school. The I 8 became the Signal regiment S I that eventually moved to Enköping in 1982.

The huge area was re-created as a haven for research and think-tank entrepreneurs and becoming Uppsala Science Park. Uppsala University's departments of mathematics and natural sciences are located here, and the latest addition is the Ångström Laboratory. The nearby Biomedical Centre, University of Agricultural Sciences and Akademiska Hospital help to create an environment with strong and far-reaching research potential and spark creativity.

View towards Vaksala

At the end it was Walpurgis Eve, the flat county's and city's very own New Year's Eve celebration. The smoke from the fires whispered their bands over the plains into the dusk. ... When the north sky already was streaked with light, one can still see beyond the horizon, Isolated images of blistering bonfires from Bälinge and Åkerby churches like falling stars. All through the night the smell of burning tar lingers on the edges of the wind, mixed with the freshness of naked, moist earth.

The Uppsala that the child, Dag Hammarskjöld, recorded during the 1910s from his home, high above the city on Slottsbacken (castle hill) was the town of the vibrant countryside with a small radius and narrow circumference. In the villages, the bonfires burned as they had for centuries. But still in 1955, Tage Danielsson, later a comedian, needed only to lift his hand and point to emphasise the students' need for play and freedom. From his vantage point, on Slottsbacken in front of the Gunilla bell tower, he could say:

> *We want to stand and watch as the winter gives way.*
> *And far beyond Slottsbacken's contoured horizon*
> *We want to hunt a dream*
> *With this round horizon*
> *We want to be gathered like flies to the fires on the plains.*

Now we take a look at a rebuilt Kungsängen, a soon-to-be renovated central station, the low Fålhagen and the heights of Sala backar, towards the Cathedral's simple and secluded little sister, Vaksala Church. The plains are gone and the fires have died. Somewhere over there might have been a fire, long ago in Sala village, whose more northern barns may have been the birthplace of Gamla Uppsala and therefore Uppsala. Barns of a more modern type, shopping barns, have proliferated around the entrances into Uppsala but most of these are south of Uppsala along where the road to Stockholm begins.

Power and water

More and more sprawling shopping barns are being built around the southern approach to Uppsala

If you come to Uppsala from Stockholm, the first sight you will see is the central heating plant's more than 100-m tall chimney, and not the Cathedral's 118,7-m tall spires. The

smoke from the chimney stacks are gradually much more
environmentally sound.

The heating plant distributes 1 billion kWh in the
Uppsala area. Electricity consumption has doubled since
the 1970s. De-regulation of the energy supplier market in
1996 spurred local companies to sell energy throughout
all of Sweden. Most of the buildings in the city are heated
by the district heating network and a number of industries
also purchase the steam heat.

A new product is distant cooling which as of now only
is delivered to the Pfizer area. The product is obtained
from the town's wastewater which otherwise would drain
out into the Fyris River.

The Pump House next to Island's Falls near the southern
tower of the castle sufficed for many years as a water
reservoir. A new system was introduced in the 1930s
when a pump was built in Galgbacken to the north, later
partially supplemented by a water tower in the Stadsskogen
to the west, and Boländerna to the east. The almost 50-
metre tall Bolandstower up on its hill is a conspicuous
addition to the Uppsala's silhouette, but leaves a strong
impression even from nearby as a temple dedicated to the
four elements.

Register